The Amorality of Atheism

GIORGIO ROVERSI

To Alice and Laura

CONTENTS

ACKNOWLEDGMENTS

I would like to thank Andrew Kirke for critical and helpful comments in early drafts. I'm also grateful to all those - atheists, sceptics, believers - who have posted comments on *The amorality of atheism* Facebook page, unwillingly contributing to the book.

From an atheist point of view, human beings are no more than random collocations of atoms and molecules, bio-organisms whose only aim in life is to preserve and spread their genes. The only reason why we act altruistically, the only reason why we are "good" is because by doing so we enhance our chances to survive and reproduce, and pass our genes on to the next generation. In other words, when we act altruistically, we actually operate for our long-term benefit, for our self-interest. This is our "morality" according to atheism. But that begs the question: why we act against the interest of others, why are we "bad"? The answer is: for the same reason. Because by doing so we enhance our chances to survive and reproduce, and pass our genes on to the next generation. The foundation of atheistic morality is at the same time its negation. A morality based on self-interest denies itself. It simply does not exist.

Morality comes from something which transcends our genes. Transcendent, that is to say, religious. Something which cannot be scientifically proved, but is there nonetheless. We can - and often we do - go against what our genes dictate, for a reason that cannot be explained or justified in atheistic, materialistic terms, and which makes us moral beings.

CHAPTER 1

WHY WE OUGHT TO BE GOOD: THE RELIGIOUS ROOT OF MORALITY

Richard Dawkins has said often that Darwinism is a science, not an ethic. Turn natural selection into a code of conduct and you get disaster. But if asked where we get our morality from, if not from science or religion, the new atheists start to stammer. They tend to argue that ethics is obvious, which it isn't, or natural, which it manifestly isn't either, and end up vaguely hinting that this isn't their problem. Let someone else worry about it.

Rabbi Jonathan Sacks

I find your suggestion that atheists cannot be moral ludicrous to say the least, as well as offensive and patronising. It should be apparent to anyone that we don't need God to be moral. As explained by authors such as Steven Pinker, Richard Dawkins, Mark D. Hauser, Sam Harris, Richard Joyce, there is no need for a supernatural basis for morality, which is in fact a product of our genes. We are moral, we are good because it is in our self-interest to be so. We evolved to a stage where we are generous and kind towards others, because we expect them to be generous and kind to us, and by doing so we enhance our chances to survive and reproduce. It's called reciprocal altruism, a tool which increases our chances to survive and reproduce.

We act for the well-being of society, because if the whole of society is better off, we are better off.
As such can be subject to scientific enquiry and it can be established on an objective and universal basis, drawn from scientific data, without resorting to the supernatural.

The comment above is taken from an objection raised by one atheist commentator online, and betrays all too common atheist misconceptions regarding morality and its foundations.

Firstly, I've never argued that atheists cannot be moral. What I argue is that atheism implies an amoral view of reality. If God doesn't exist, you, I, each individual on the planet lives in an amoral Universe, in which morality does not, and cannot, exist. To use an expression from atheist philosopher Michael Ruse, morality is "an illusion". The source, the objective foundation of our morals - everybody's morals, atheists, agnostics, sceptics, believers - is ultimately grounded in the existence of a higher moral order, found in God.

Let us consider the commentator's central claim, what he regards as a perfectly reasonable, materialistic explanation for morality: "We are moral, we are good because it is in our self-interest to be so." This argument is vitiated by a fundamental flaw. And it is this: answering the question "Why are we good?" doesn't tell us anything at all about morality. For an embarrassingly obvious reason: we are not only "good", we are also "bad"; we act against the interest of others. Why? Because it is in our self-interest to be so. If self-interest is the only possible reason prompting me to be "good", self-interest is at the same time what prompts me to be "bad", to act against the interest of others.

The problem is to establish the reason why we *ought* to

be good, regardless of our self-interest. Here is where the atheist view fails. From an atheistic perspective, there is no reason why we *ought* to be good, regardless of our self-interest. Saying that human beings are mostly good is simply a descriptive statement that doesn't tell us anything at all about morality, about why we *ought* to be good [1].

When the commentator says that people ought to act for the well-being of society because it is their self-interest, since they are part of society, he implicitly acknowledges that self-interest is the only reason why people ought to act for the well-being of society. But self-interest is also the reason why people act in their own interest, and against the interests of others, against the well-being of society. Clearly this is circular reasoning.

Richard Dawkins' *The God Delusion* (2006) offers a striking example of this fallacy. The title of the chapter devoted to the topic of morality reads: "Why we are good, the root of morality". Clearly the title should have been "Why we ought to be good, the root of morality".

But the whole body of literature the commentator has referred to is guilty of committing the same error. Hauser, Pinker, Dennet and Harris each fill thousands of pages of data drawn from cognitive science, anthropology and biology, explaining why human beings tend to be generous, kind, amiable towards neighbours and friends, as well as strangers. In other words, they explain why human beings are "moral", but yet simultaneously fail to address the essential question of morality: why human beings ought to be "good", "moral", regardless of whether this action furthers their own self-interest. The reason is of course because, on an atheistic world view, there is no answer to this question.

An example might help to clarify the point. Consider the following. A politician is being offered a hefty bribe, let's say a million. Why should he not accept it? The commentator's answer to such a question would be: "Because if he rejects the bribe, the whole of society is better off; and since he is part of society he acts for his self-interest. Moreover, he will not risk going to jail, which is also in his self-interest". This is on its face true.

But here is the thing: by accepting the bribe our politician also operates for his own benefit, for his self-interest, whilst at the same time harming the whole of society.

The politician is faced with two options. The first is to accept the bribe and have a million in his bank account. By doing so he damages society and operates for his own benefit, for his self-interest. The second option is to reject the bribe. In this case he operates for the interest of the society in which he lives, therefore indirectly he also acts for his self-interest.

However, in the first case he secures a direct, immediate, substantial benefit, well worth the risk. In the second case he achieves an indirect, remote, minimal benefit. Now, if maximising the benefit is the sole and ultimate criterion that directs human behaviour, why should our politician not decide on the course of action that best serves his self-interest, even if this means acting against the interests of others? Why should he not choose the first option, which clearly is the most rational and logical, because it is the most profitable? If self-interest is what makes him abide by the rules, why shouldn't self-interest justify breaking the rules? From an atheistic point of view, there is no answer to this question. This is the amorality of atheism.

If self-interest is the only possible reason that makes a person "moral", self-interest is at the same time what makes that person "immoral", what makes him or her act against the interest of others. Indeed, on this understanding, the terms "moral" and "immoral" become meaningless. The politician taking a bribe, or the person dumping toxic waste in the river, or the banker making millions by defrauding his customers, are all just doing what their genes dictate: maximising the benefits of their actions. There is no "moral" choice, only a choice as to the course of action which best serves one's self-interest.

At this point it would be remiss not to mention a quote that epitomises the astonishing degree of inconsistency and self-contradiction of the atheist position. It is taken from Richard Dawkins' earlier work, *The Selfish Gene* (1976): "Let us try to teach generosity and altruism, because we are born selfish. Let us understand what our own selfish genes are up to, because we may then at least have the chance to upset their designs".

Obviously Dawkins belongs to that category of people who love their ideas but hate their consequences. He is perfectly aware that the only logical and coherent outcome of atheism is an amoral view of human nature, and glosses over this uncomfortable truth by preaching: "Let us not follow our selfish genes". But why not? We are our genes, our entire being is determined and defined by our genes, nothing else but our genes. It logically follows that there is no reason, in atheistic terms, to go against what our genes dictate. If you deny our spiritual dimension what is left is the bare reality of our genes. If you claim that there exists a reason for our actions that transcends our genes, you acknowledge a transcendent, religious foundation to morality. If you believe that a human being is something more than a bunch of cells and his actions are determined by something else rather than their genes, you are by definition a believer.

We can go beyond our genes because we are other than our genes. We can go against what our genes dictate, because there is a reason for our actions that transcends our material selves, and makes us moral beings.

CHAPTER 2

THE ATHEIST DOGMA:
A MORALITY WITHOUT GOD

Science must not impose any philosophy,
any more than the telephone must tell us what to say.

G.K.Chesterton

Morality must be regarded as an un-developed branch of science and as such be the subject of scientific enquiry. Matter is all there is, therefore any moral judgment must be based on hard facts, verifiable evidence, on objective truth discovered by scientific research, which is the only rational approach. To imagine a foundation to morality as something that is scientifically unverifiable equates to adopting an irrational position.

In considering this claim, it seems clear that the opposite is true. It is irrational, delusional and intellectually dishonest to pretend, against all the evidence, that morality can have a foundation other than a religious one. It is reason that leads us to acknowledge the basic, verifiable fact that – from an atheistic perspective – morality does not exist. Far from defeating reason, to acknowledge the supernatural, transcendent, scientifically unprovable foundation of morality is the only rational approach to it.

Morality is not, and never will be, a branch of science,

however developed. For the reasons already explained: science can, in some ways, assist a politician, or a banker, or any of us, in determining how to better pursue our self-interest, but it does not in any way offer any ultimate reasons for why we ought not act against the interest of others, or for the well-being of society. And it never will.

Science describes, it does not make moral judgments. As atheist Alfred Kinsey – who not surprisingly devoted his entire life to the task of making Christian morality, or rather morality tout court, a thing of the past – declared, "we are the recorders and reporters of facts - not the judges of the behaviors we describe".

As an atheist, the only reasonable and coherent position is to describe behaviour, not to judge it. The atheist can attempt to determine by scientific means on the course of actions that will deliver the best results in materialistic terms, but he cannot define those actions as "moral" or "immoral". His point of view is, in fact, amoral. To claim that science can determine moral values is an ideological position, not a scientific one. By doing so, he masquerades as science what is in fact blind, prejudiced dogmatism. Morality without God is the entrenched dogma, the unproved assumption of the atheist.

In a late U-turn, perhaps after realising the inherent fallacy of the notion of morality "discovered by scientific research", our atheist commentator protests: "Why is the burden of proof on me? Why should I have to provide scientific evidence to my claim that morality can exist without God?" The answer seems fairly obvious. The atheist is the one claiming that scientific inquiry can be and must be applied to moral questions. The atheist is the one claiming that morality can be based on scientific data rather than grounded in our understanding of God.

Hence the burden of proof lies with the atheist. The onus is on the atheist to demonstrate that there is a reason, grounded in scientific evidence, to go against what our genes dictate; a reason why we ought to be good, regardless of our self-interest. No proof means that a supposed "morality without God", "based on hard facts" and "verifiable evidence", is in fact, as mentioned, an atheist dogma.

CHAPTER 3

COMPASSION

*Without religion the coherence of an ethic of compassion
cannot be established.
The principle of respect for persons
and the principle of the survival of the fittest
are mutually exclusive.*

R. Z. Friedman, philosopher at the University of Toronto

*Empathy, compassion towards our fellow human beings, the innate
urge to share the sufferings of others are a common trait in human
nature. We feel good if we help others, we feel bad if we harm them. I
believe that compassion is the basis of morality.*

If more evidence was needed of how the atheist's
convictions are not based on hard facts and rigorous
logical reasoning, but rather on entirely emotional and
irrational factors, here we have it.

Empathy, compassion are feelings, the atheist says. To be
precise, they are chemical reactions that take place within
our organisms. We assist the sick, we feed the hungry or
we clothe the poor simply because a chemical reaction
induces us to do so. That's all. Our sense of right or wrong
is – according to our atheist – a product of chemical

reactions. And a chemical reaction is neither moral or immoral, it simply occurs. Is our atheist commentator seriously suggesting that a feeling, a chemical reaction in our organism, can be the basis of morality?

It is true that empathy and compassion are a common trait in human nature, but so are greed, anger, hatred, lust and thirst for power. An atheistic-materialistic worldview derives no reason why compassion or empathy should be esteemed over any other human feeling. A tyrant might "feel good" killing and torturing people, for so long as this keeps him in power. But does this "good feeling" make him moral?

In Euripides's play, Medea avenges her husband's betrayal by slaying their children [2]. On an atheistic worldview, why shouldn't her devouring feelings of hatred and revenge against her husband prevail over the impulse to love and protect her children?

On what basis would the atheist determine that any given feeling, something produced by no more than a chemical reaction taking place within our organism, is morally more appreciable than any other? On the basis of another feeling? Itself a product of random chemical reactions? How can one establish which feeling, which "urge", is morally right? The answer is that one can't, unless one resorts to something other than "feeling"" as an arbiter for moral judgment.

On the atheistic worldview, why would compassion, pity of other peoples' suffering be a good thing? Why not embrace Friedrich Nietzsche's view that:

> Pity runs counter to the law of development, which is the law of selection. Pity preserves things that are ripe for decline, it defends things that have been

disowned and condemned by life, and it gives a depressive and questionable character to life itself by keeping alive an abundance of failures of every type. People have dared to call pity a virtue... people have gone even further, making it into the virtue, the foundation and source of all virtues.[3]

In a godless world, logic is on Nietzsche's side. And yet the atheist incoherently and emotionally appeals to compassion as a foundation upon which morality can be based. By doing so, he unwittingly borrows from his religious heritage – presumably Christian – adopting a concept that in atheistic terms is meaningless.

Compassion is indeed the essence of morality, because it is something more and entirely other than a mere feeling. The "urge to share the sufferings of others" has moral significance, it is a moral value, precisely because it is more than just a chemical reaction, but something that pre-exists and transcends us and our material reality.

CHAPTER 4

MEANING AND MORALITY

Camus has been rightly criticized for inconsistently holding both to the absurdity of life and the ethics of human love and brotherhood. The two are logically incompatible. Bertrand Russell, too, was inconsistent. For though he was an atheist, he was an outspoken social critic, denouncing war and restrictions on sexual freedom. Russell admitted that he could not live as though ethical values were simply a matter of personal taste, and that he therefore found his own views "incredible." "I do not know the solution," he confessed. The point is that if there is no God, then objective right and wrong cannot exist. As Dostoyevsky said, "All things are permitted."

William Lane Craig

I believe it is a sign of arrogance to presume that the universe was created with "you" in mind". Of course it is unpleasant to think that we come from nothing and drift into nothingness, but we must face the crude, uncomfortable truth that we live in a meaningless universe in which we are negligible, irrelevant accidents. To delude ourselves into believing that we are anything else is a luxury we cannot afford.

I'm amazed at how our atheist fails to recognise, as most atheists do, a macroscopical contradiction in his position. It is of course perfectly logical and coherent for an atheist to maintain that we live in a meaningless, purposeless universe in which "we are negligible, irrelevant accidents".

However, the contradiction resides in assuming that in a universe merely governed by the laws of physics, our existence and our actions have any moral relevance.

It is astonishingly incoherent and illogical to claim in one breath that we are "negligible, irrelevant accident", that our existence and actions are meaningless, that we are a product of chance, that we come from nothing and we are destined to drift into nothingness, and at the same time to contend that we are "moral" beings.

It is absurd and self-contradictory to declare that it is a sign of arrogance to presume the universe was created with "us" in mind, and then to claim that random collocations of molecules which constitute we human beings can be capable of moral obligations.

As Milan Kundera reminds us in the novel *The Unbearable Lightness of Being* (1984), one cannot condemn the ephemeral. And man, in our atheist's view, is ephemeral. Man is a "negligible, irrelevant accident" that cannot be judged or condemned. On the atheist perspective, observes Peter Hitchens, "we are no more than a meaningless accident, living in the midst of another meaningless accident, and in which our actions are of no significance beyond their immediate effect". [4]

Reality as our atheist portrays it is not only meaningless, it is amoral. In his essay *Ends and Means* (1937) atheist Aldous Huxley explains:

> I had motives for not wanting the world to have a meaning; consequently assumed that it had none, and was able without any difficulty to find satisfying reasons for this assumption. The philosopher who

finds no meaning in the world is not concerned exclusively with a problem in metaphysics, he is also concerned to prove that there is no valid reason why he personally should not do as he wants to do, or why his friends should not seize political power and govern in the way that they find most advantageous to themselves... For myself, the philosophy of meaningless was essentially an instrument of liberation, sexual and political.

Our atheist friend, like most atheists (Huxley being one exception), loves to depict himself as liberated and free from the delusions with which the theist must grapple, an emboldened soul daring to stare over into the abyss of meaninglessness. But yet, his real motive for choosing non-belief over belief in God is rather more prosaic: in a nutshell, he sees "no valid reason why he personally should not do as he wants to do".

Our atheist claims that to believe we are not negligible, irrelevant accidents, but that we are instead created, willed and loved by God is a sign of arrogance and "a luxury we cannot afford". My answer to that is: of course it is a luxury we can afford, because is a gift. And surely it is not a sign of arrogance to accept it.

CHAPTER 5

MORAL RELATIVISM
AND THE FALSE DOUBTS OF THE
ATHEIST

Someone who says that there are no truths,
or that all truth is 'merely relative,'
is asking you not to believe him. So don't.

Roger Scruton

Perhaps there is no objective morality, but there is nonetheless a subjective morality. You can have your morals, without expecting everyone else to adhere to your standard of right or wrong. The assertion of an absolute moral truth, accessible only to believers is evidence of the inherently violent nature of religion. On the other hand, the secular approach – atheists', agnostics', secular humanists' - propounds doubt, including moral doubt, not absolute moral truth; therefore they are compelled to constantly question their own convictions and to accept dialogue, being content with momentary truths.

Our atheist's statement here strikes me not only as antithetical to his earlier position (claiming that there is "an objective morality based on scientific data", remember?), but also as hypocritical.

Moral relativism has always been an easily refutable, self-defeating philosophy, not least because the very concept of subjective morality is a contradiction in terms. A "morality" where everybody is only subjectively moral, is also a morality where everybody is subjectively immoral. Logically this means no morality at all. By rejecting absolute moral truth, our atheist implicitly denies the very notion of morality itself.

But what I find to be particularly hypocritical and dishonest is the suggestion that secularism is synonym for "doubt" and "tolerance", as opposed to the certainty and intolerance of religion.

From the time of the French Revolution, secularism, when translated into social or political action, has hardly been a synonym for tolerance and scepticism, but has been instead unfailingly characterised by a presumption to occupy the moral high ground which entitles to deal out moral judgments. This self-righteousness has often extended to such a point that its proponents have not hesitated to execute those who dare to dissent from the new received orthodoxy, with an unwavering certainty that they are fulfilling the momentous mission of promoting social and moral progress.

It is perhaps worth remembering that Communism – an ideological monster responsible for, within just a few short decades, mass murders on a scale previously unprecedented in human history – is a political manifestation of the idea of a secular society. Marxist communist ideologies are intrinsically linked to the notion of a state sponsored, and enforced, secularism [5]. Communism has never struck me as particularly tolerant or imbued with scepticism. It is indeed a shame that the ruthless dictators of state atheism – such as Stalin, Mao and Pol Pot - before butchering tens of millions of people, did not doubt for an instant they were doing the right thing.

But even in today's Western society, secularism invariably results in the obsessive, fanatical judgmentalism of political correctness, which never doubts the righteousness of its position and does not brook dissent. Those who dare to disagree are identified as enemies that need demonising and destroying, by any possible means, often to the extent of legitimising physical and verbal violence.

This dissonance between boasted scepticism and actual moralistic intransigence is nowhere more manifest than in academia. In *The Closing of the American Mind* (1987), Allan Bloom observes: "There is one thing a professor can be absolutely certain of: almost every student entering the university believes, or says he believes, that truth is relative."

And yet the same students are likely to be committed ideologues unshakable in their beliefs, hardly subjecting their position to the sort of scrutiny reserved for religious belief, and regarding any criticism of secular orthodoxy as a thought crime [6].

The display of moral outrage towards ideas that don't fit the secular narrative and the tendency to suppress free speech have become a constant feature in university campuses across America and Europe. Conservative speakers are routinely denied a platform, and any opinion perceived as a threat to the prevailing secular dogma is marginalized or censored altogether.

What appears increasingly obvious is that the "moral doubt" praised by secularists, far from being a coherent philosophical stance, is merely an expedient to attack religious belief; a selective scepticism that corrodes religious faith, but leaves secular dogmas intact.

The secular worldview doesn't compel you constantly to "question your own convictions and to accept dialogue, being content with momentary truths"; it simply allows you to dispose of the truth you don't like and replace it with your own "truth".

The result is the rise of political correctness, a secular pseudo-morality, which is a delusional attempt to fill the moral vacuum with the multiplication of rules designed to control speech and thought [7]. As G.K. Chesterton warned with remarkable prescience, "If men will not be governed by the Ten Commandments, they shall be governed by the ten thousand commandments".

If "the truth will set you free" (John 8:32), the rejection of truth - its disintegration into a myriad of "momentary truths" - will make you a slave to ideological trends, and therefore to the prevailing cultural and political powers.

CHAPTER 6

THE SELF-RIGHTEOUS ATHEIST

The man of this school goes first to the political meeting, where he complains that savages are treated as if they were beasts; then he takes his hat and umbrella and goes on to a scientific meeting, where he proves they practically are beasts ... In his book on politics he attacks men for trampling on morality; in his book on ethics he attacks morality for trampling on men.

G.K. Chesterton

I'm an atheist and I consider myself to be a moral person, guided by nothing other than my own conscience. In fact, I think I am morally superior to most believers. And to be perfectly honest, I believe that a modern, enlightened society could do without people who seek moral guidance in Bronze Age Myths.

Our atheist has here provided me with a perfect example of the inconsistency and hypocrisy I was referring to earlier. He states that there is no such a thing as "absolute moral truth" and that whoever claims otherwise is intolerant, and in the same breath describes himself as "morally superior", implying that "absolute moral truth" (of which presumably he is the sole arbiter and interpreter) does indeed exist.

This apparently puzzling incoherence has in fact a very

simple explanation. Our atheist possesses an unshakeable confidence in his own righteousness. The reason for this is obvious: he is his own absolute source of morality, and sets his own moral standards, by which he judges both himself and everyone else. As Peter Hitchens observes, "Unlike Christians, atheists have a high opinion of their own nature" [8]. It becomes terribly easy to feel virtuous when you are the one defining virtue. Our atheist cannot recognise his own moral inadequacy without a moral standard that transcends him. He could never declare, with the prophet Isaiah, that in the face of a moral standard set by a morally perfect God, "all our righteous works are as filthy rags" (Isaiah 64:6).

Our atheist contends that he is guided by his conscience. But what he calls conscience is in fact the voice of his genes – as he implicitly admitted –, a mere alibi that is summoned to condone every instinct, every urge, every desire, a puppet tribunal , in which he serves as judge and jury, and before which he will always be declared "not guilty". Atheism allows our atheist to create his own moral standards, which are, as Nietzsche would say, "beyond good and evil".

The biblical story of Adam and Eve gives what is arguably the most sublime depiction of the farcical "morality" of the atheist. It portraits the seminal, ancestral temptation to do away with God and his law, to dethrone Him, to set ourselves up to be like Him. "You will be like God, knowing good and evil", voiced the serpent, as he tempted Eve to turn her back on her Creator (Genesis, 3:5).

To know good and evil means to arrogate to ourselves the power to define good and evil, and as a result to be beyond good and evil, to set our own moral standards. The ultimate transgression is not to break the rules, but to set yourself up as the ruler. To the believer morality preexisted man, it is a given, that which is fixed and immutable, grounded in the very nature and essence of Him from whom all things flow. Conversely, on the atheist view, man is the supreme arbiter, and morality is subject to manipulation at man's own discretion.

Perhaps that is why our atheist finds, as he said at the beginning, intolerably "offensive and patronising" the notion that there cannot be a morality without God. The very idea of a transcendent, external, pre-existent morality, the thought that, when it comes to defining good and evil there is a higher authority than himself , challenges his position on the moral "high ground", and threatens to topple him from the moral pedestal that he has erected and placed himself upon.

And there is, of course, an obvious consequence to this. As our atheist feels morally superior, he also feels entitled to recreate society and its structure by reinventing its moral code; to invent a Utopia made in the image of a "superior moral standard" (one which is of course his standard). And, I suppose, he also feels in a position to decide who deserves to live (according to Richard Dawkins, those affected by Down syndrome don't) [9], or meets the minimum requirements to become a worthy member of this perfect society (it's easy to guess that in it there could hardly be any role or place for those who don't share your "modern, enlightened" views, or "who seek moral guidance in Bronze Age Myths").

Atheism, in its amorality, grants the atheist the dream of a society entirely manufactured by man – by the "modern", "enlightened" man – and this is what makes it so appealing, so intellectually desirable to the western, secularised intellectual. Not its rigorous logic – or rather the lack of it – but the illusion that by embracing it, one is creating a brave new world, where the old, divine order is replaced by the new.

CHAPTER 7

ATHEISM AND TOTALITARIANISM

Dostoevsky wrote that in a future day men would say there is no crime, there is no sin, there is no guilt, there is only hunger; then men will come crying and fawning at our feet saying to us, "Give us bread." Nothing will matter except the economic.

A spirit of license makes a man refuse to commit himself to any standards. The right time is the way he sets his watch. The yardstick has the number of inches that he wills it to have. Liberty becomes license and unbounded license leads to unbounded tyranny. When society reaches this stage, and there is no standard of right and wrong outside of the individual himself, then the individual is defenseless against the onslaughts of cruder and more violent men who proclaim their own subjective sense of values. Once my idea of morality is just as good as your idea of morality, then the morality that is going to prevail is the morality that is stronger.

Bishop Fulton J. Sheen

There needn't be a reason why people ought not to act in their self-interest, even when is against the interest of others. People would just have to buy into it. And if they don't, the state must ensure that the individual does not act against the interest of society, as well as impose moral education amongst the young.

In a few words – perhaps unconsciously – our atheist has made two crucial admissions.

The first is his tacit reaffirmation that a morality without God does not in fact exist, since on an atheist perspective there is no reason "why people ought not to act in their self-interest, even when is against the interest of others". This makes the suggestion that the state must "impose moral education amongst the young" (on the basis of a morality that doesn't exist) slightly risible. Moral education – which is somewhat different from indoctrination – critically means presenting the ultimate, transcendent reason for our actions. Precisely what atheism is unable to offer.

Secondly, our atheist has also tacitly affirmed the inherently totalitarian nature of atheism. The state – he says – must ensure that the individual does not act against the interest of others, or the whole of society. Precisely. Since on the atheistic world view there is no morality – and therefore no ultimate, transcendent reason why people ought not to act in their self-interest - the state takes upon itself the role of sole factor which ensures, by force or by threat of force, that the individual does not act against the interest of others. In other words, the state has to be totalitarian.

Perhaps the most accurate illustration of this chilling world view is found in a verse from the poem *The Rock* (1934) by T.S. Eliot:

> They constantly try to escape
> From the darkness outside and within
> By dreaming of systems so perfect that no one will need to be good.

The totalitarian state is, in the amoral atheistic Zeitgeist, the "perfect system" which aims to neutralise the risk ingrained in the individual's moral choice and ensures that he, willingly or not, acts in the interest of society. It is the "perfect system" whereby the Samaritan is forced to act in the interest of others, and therefore he does not need to be "good" or "moral", because morality no longer exists. The totalitarian state is the "perfect system" that encourages more and more, and might in the near future impose, through eugenics – "good" (eu-) "genes" – for instance through selective abortion, to artificially pre-determine human nature and behaviour, and to force the individual to contain selfish urges and become a tame social animal (Stanley Kubrick's *Clockwork Orange* [10] springs to mind).

This grim vision is a logical, inevitable consequence of the assumption that human nature is inherently amoral, incapable of transcending its materiality, its biological structure, and therefore it can only be constrained by a "perfect system", which is in fact the totalitarian state (of which communist regimes that plagued the 20th century were but one possible manifestation). A state that not only compels the individual to behave "morally", but defines what is "moral", assumes the position of ultimate and exclusive source of morality, of final arbiter of justice and truth, right and wrong (where "moral" becomes synonym for legal) and arbitrarily determines the value, or non-value, of the individual.

Such a state would be but the projection of contingent material interests of the prevailing political and economic forces, whether that be the expression of the majority or that of a powerful and wealthy elite. As Alexis de Tocqueville prophesied in *Democracy in America* (1835), "Despotism may govern without faith, but liberty cannot". The moral vacuum created by the exclusion of religion is fatally filled by the coercion of totalitarian state. If material self-interest determines human behaviour, the bond is as tenuous and fragile as the interest in question. But if the social bond has a sacred, religious element that transcends the interest of the individuals involved, it remains unaffected (the term religion, after all, comes from the Latin *religare*, "to bind together").

It is no coincidence that every civilisation in human history has recognised at its foundation an element of sacredness, to which the civil authority is ultimately bound. The sacred is an awareness of moral boundaries that are not circumscribed by us, of an ultimate reason that cannot be found in us. It is the realisation that what binds us together as a society is something that lies beyond ourselves, and that human beings have an inherent value that cannot be arbitrarily limited or denied by political, economic or social power.

A final note. Our atheist inadvertently exposes as a modern canard the idea that atheism offers an optimistic view of human nature (remember the myth of the *noble savage?*), as opposed to the pessimistic religious view of human nature. In reality, the opposite is true. It is precisely atheism which cultivates the bleak notion that human beings have no reason to go against what their genes dictate, because they are nothing more than their genes, and that they are unable to act "morally" (since morality does not exist), but simply choose a course of action that best serves their self-interest.

Indeed our atheist's statement betrays a manifest mistrust towards human nature, inherently amoral, incapable of transcending its materiality, and therefore in need of coercion by a "perfect system", the totalitarian state.

On the other hand, optimism towards human nature comes from the belief that human beings are not merely steadfast agents of their genes, but they are spiritual, as well as material, entities. It is not a delusional, utopistic and ultimately false optimism, based on the denial of the reality of evil, but based on the conviction that human nature, imperfect and inadequate, can be overcome and transformed by supernature, by transcendence.

CHAPTER 8

THE CHRISTIAN PARADOX

...we preach Christ crucified:
a stumbling block to Jews and foolishness to Gentiles

1 Corinthians 1:23

Plurality of faiths is an insurmountable obstacle to the recognition of a transcendent foundation to morality. If we accept that the existence of morality is dependent on the existence of a deity, to which deity, or deities, should I resort to? Why should I believe that Christianity is the true faith? Why would God be the Christian God? What makes Christianity an exception amongst thousands of religious beliefs?

As an argument to deny the transcendent root of morality, "plurality of faiths" is remarkably bad. It is a glaring fallacy to presume that difficulty of enquiry implies that it is impossible to know the truth, or that truth does not exist. The argument would make as much sense as to say that not knowing the way to London, or the fact that there is more than one way to get to London, is proof that London does not exist.

This argument appears to me to be an awkward attempt to divert the focus away from the main topic of our discussion, the fact that "morality without God" does not exist. I could be an atheist, an agnostic, a Hindu, a Muslim, a Buddhist, and I would still be bound to acknowledge that there is no morality without God. Because to recognise this fact – as I've already pointed out – is an act of rationality and intellectual honesty, not an act of faith.

But our atheist asks me why Christianity would be the true faith, why it would be an exception amongst thousands of religious beliefs. My answer is: because Christianity is a paradox. It is the inconceivable – absurd by merely human standards – claim that God chooses to share the sufferings of His creatures, by becoming a vulnerable, innocent victim. It is the belief that God "took our infirmities and bore our diseases" (Matthew 8:17), and consented to be betrayed, abandoned, imprisoned, mocked, spat upon, tortured, and put to death, nailed to a cross like a low criminal. And three days later rose again. This is what makes Christianity exceptional. And true.

A God who were a mere product of our fantasies would not be on a cross, would not be compassionate, suffering with us. There's an interesting episode narrated in the Gospels of the Passion where the chief priests and the scribes challenge Jesus to prove Himself to be God and come down from the cross, so "that we may see and believe" (Mark 15:32). It is a perfect depiction of the human, all too human idea of deity as mere projection of the urge to follow the genes' imperative to survive and avoid suffering. This is precisely what Christianity is not.

Earlier our atheist recognised compassion as the basis of morality. But, as I pointed out, by doing so he unwittingly borrows from his culture's Christian heritage a concept that in atheistic terms is meaningless. If compassion is the basis of morality, "the foundation and source of all virtues", it is not just a chemical reaction in our organisms, but rather part of something that comes before us and transcends us, the reason why we can go against what our genes dictate. The Cross is the manifestation of that reason. The Cross tells us that the absurdity, the foolishness of compassion is in fact the reasonableness of God. It tells us that self-sacrifice, sharing in the suffering of others is indeed the basis of morality, because God, the source of and reason for all things, has become flesh and blood, and shared with us in our sufferings.

> For we do not have a high priest who is unable to sympathise with our weaknesses, but one who in every respect has been tempted as we are, yet without sin. (Hebrews 4:15)

The Cross is the paradigm of human morality, the triumph of our spiritual dimension over the dictatorship of our genes, our selfish nature. It is the assertion that we are not defined by our genes, or our sinful hearts, that morality is not the product of what our genes dictate, or our selfish urges desire, but instead a fruit of the Spirit.

If God exists, He went to the Cross. That is why I am a Christian.

CHAPTER 9

MORALITY AND FEAR

Atheism is a fairy tale
for people afraid of the light

John Lennox

Who just blindly obeys the orders of a celestial dictator or Big Brother deity because of fear of punishment or promise of a reward in an afterlife is not moral at all. Only the atheist can be moral, since he is truly free to choose his actions, without hope of reward or fear of punishment. Atheists don't need to be scared or bribed into goodness.

Our atheist's depiction of religious morality as simply "obeying the orders of a celestial dictator or Big Brother deity" strikes me as a textbook example of the superficial, derisory and invariably flawed approach that characterises New Atheism. Rather than seeking rational enquiry and debate, he is stereotyping and presenting a distorted image, a caricature of religious morality; of Christian morality to be precise, since he is addressing a Christian.

Let me firstly point out the irony of the suggestion that "only the atheist can be moral, since he is really free to act". Our atheist does not seem to realise that the very concept of acting freely is entirely incompatible with the atheistic-materialistic view that our actions are determined only by our genes, and nothing else but our genes. It is precisely in his view that "goodness" is only a product of bribery. We are good because our genes tell us it is convenient to be good. We are bribed into goodness by our genes, in the hope of a material reward. We are not free to choose our actions, we are not "moral", we just do what our genes dictate. It is his view, rather than the Christian's, that requires a dictatorship: the dictatorship of genes. It is his view that is based on the assumption human nature is inherently amoral, incapable of transcending its materiality, its biological structure (since only matter exists), and therefore can only be constrained by fear of punishment, prime examples of which – as I pointed out previously – are found in the nightmarishly oppressive regimes produced by atheism in the 20th century. For man to have a moral ability or freedom presupposes that he has a reason to go against what his genes dictate, to transcend his materiality or to act other than in his self-interest. This reason exists, but the atheist does not like it. It's called God.

Previously I mentioned that our atheist's summary is a caricature of Christian morality rather than a true representation. Indeed, I have yet to meet a Christian (I wouldn't presume to speak for those of other religious beliefs) whose notion of God coincides with that of a "celestial dictator or Big Brother deity", whatever that might be, and who would subscribe to our atheist's definition of Christian morality as "blindly obeying orders".

A Christian is someone who believes that the ultimate, transcendent reason for his actions - his morality - is not something obscure and distant, but has become immanent, has become one of us, has revealed itself as infinite love in the person of Jesus Christ. A Christian is Zaccheus, a corrupt tax collector, who suddenly decides to "give half of his possessions to the poor", and if he "cheated anybody out of anything" will "pay back four times the amount" (Luke 19:8), not because is stricken with fear or "blindly obeys orders", but because he has finally met, on a street of Jericho, the infinite love that created him, the ultimate reason to be something other than a corrupt tax collector serving his own self-interest. A Christian is Mary Magdalene, a prostitute, who washes Jesus feet with her tears and dries them with her hair, not out of fear of a celestial dictator, but out of a reciprocal love of the infinite love that sees beyond her materiality, her weaknesses and her faults. "For love of Thy love I do it; reviewing my most wicked ways" [11] writes Saint Augustine explaining his obedience to the commands of God.

In Greek mythology, Odysseus, the hero of Homer's Odyssey, was curious as to the nature of the Sirens' song. On the advice of Circe, a goddess of magic, he had his sailors plug their ears with beeswax and tie him to the mast. He ordered his men to leave him tied tightly to the mast, no matter how much he would beg. Yet when he heard their song, he ordered the sailors to untie him.

This response characterises that of those who are motivated to obedience in God by fear. The call or allure of sin will always be greater than the chains which bind them, so no true obedience lies in their hearts.

Continuing the analogy, the response of Christians to God is closer to that of Orpheus, who, when he heard the sirens' voices, drew his lyre and played music that was louder and more beautiful, drowning out the Sirens' bewitching songs.

Beyond parody and caricature, a response such as this characterises what morality is to a Christian: the encounter between God's infinite, unfailing love, and man's limited, imperfect love, and a call to morality far greater than the power exerted over our hearts by our selfish genes.

CHAPTER 10

CHRISTIAN SECULARISTS

…if the salt loses its saltiness,
how can it be made salty again?
It is no longer good for anything,
except to be thrown out and trampled underfoot.

Matthew 5:13

I don't deny that Jesus Christ can be regarded as a great moral teacher. But so was Confucius, who taught - five centuries before Christ – "Do not unto another that you would not have him do unto you. Thou needest this law alone. It is the foundation of all the rest." This is the Golden Rule on which I believe our morality should be based upon.
I don't have a problem with Christianity per se, rather with your fundamentalist, exclusivist approach. And I admire moderate, liberal Christians who are more concerned with social justice and the protection of the environment than theological diatribes, as you seem to be.

Our atheist's words remind me of an aphorism by Colombian philosopher Nicolas Gomez Davila: "Overstated admiration for Jesus Christ as a moral teacher immediately betrays the atheist" [12]. It also betrays - I should add - a Christian who is indistinguishable from an atheist. But I will further comment on that in a moment.

Let me first explain why our atheist's premise – "the Golden Rule on which I believe our morality should be based upon" – is deeply flawed. He falls into what can be defined as the "Golden Rule fallacy", which is this. Saying that morality is based on the rule "Do unto others as you would have them do unto you", or indeed any rule, is a meaningless and baseless assertion unless we are able to give a reason why we ought to "Do unto others as you would have them do unto us". In other words, foundation to morality is not a rule - however "golden"- but is the ultimate reason why we ought to act according to that rule. Anyone can claim that a certain rule must be followed, but the claim is meaningless unless one is able to offer the ultimate reason why we ought to follow that rule. A reason that can only be found in transcendence: precisely what the atheistic world view cannot offer. This is the unique and irreplaceable role of religion: to offer the ultimate, transcendent reason for our actions, thus providing a foundation to morality.

Which brings me to the next point. Our atheist friend states that Jesus Christ can be regarded as a great moral teacher. As C.S. Lewis famously noted, this is the one thing we must not say, because a man who was merely a man and said the sort of things Jesus said would not be a great moral teacher, but a lunatic [13]. Jesus made himself "equal with God" (John 5:18) and even went so far as to use the very words by which God revealed Himself to Moses from the burning bush (John 8:58). Indeed, Jesus was put to death not because he upheld a radically alternative set of moral principles - in which case he would merely have had a pleasant discussion with Scribes and High Priests on the exegesis of scriptures -, but because He identified Himself with the ultimate reason for those principles, thus affirming His divinity.

Christianity is in fact the religion that identifies in Jesus the ultimate reason for our moral principles, for our "Golden" rules. To quote John's Gospel, He is the Logos of God, the Reason for all things made flesh. "I am the way and the truth and the life. No one comes to the Father except through me" (John 14:6). A rather "fundamentalist", "exclusivist approach", I would say. But this is the core belief of Christianity, which our atheist friend does seem to have a problem with. Anything else is its politically correct parody.

I said that overstated admiration for Jesus Christ as a moral teacher betrays a Christian who is indistinguishable from an atheist. This is, I believe, the key to understanding the phenomenon of secularisation and de-Christianisation that has swept Western society in the last few decades. At the root of secularisation is not merely the non-belief in the existence of God, but the acceptance of the atheist dogma of a morality without God, of a set of moral values, of "Golden Rules" independent from God, from Christ, who therefore becomes irrelevant.

Christians in the West have not only passively endured a process of secularisation; they've actively promoted it, insofar as they've adopted the secular notion that morality can exist without God.

The "moderate", "progressive", "liberal Christians", "concerned with social justice and the protection of the environment", who see the Gospel simply as a 'Handbook' for 'Moral Guidance', and the divinity of Christ as a cause of embarrassment, an unnecessary occasion of disagreement with atheists and people of other faiths, have reduced the Church to a campaigning force for social justice, indistinguishable from secular organisations, de facto annulling the social, cultural and political relevance of

Christianity.

It's no wonder our atheist friend admires them. They have in a way succeeded where even the most zealous militant atheists have failed.

CHAPTER 11

SECULARISATION
AND THE CULTURE WAR

It is a cultural war, as critical to the kind of nation we shall be
as was the Cold War itself,
for this war is for the soul of America.

Patrick J. Buchanan

However strongly your fundamentalist instincts resist the idea of a non-religious society, the reality is that secularism is on the winning side of history. Secularisation is the natural and inevitable end result of a modern society that wants to leave behind superstition and irrationality. Religion is dying in the West because it is something the modern, developed, technologically advanced world has grown out of. Certain views are no longer acceptable and have no place in the public sphere. The portion of population describing themselves as non-believers is rapidly growing. And perhaps more importantly, the central tenets of secularism – such as separation between state and religion, neutrality of the state - are now widely accepted even amongst believers.

The widespread view that secularisation is a spontaneous, inevitable phenomenon, the necessary and unavoidable fate of a modern society, is one of the most enduring myths of our age [14].

It is unquestionable that Western society, and Europe in particular, over the span of only few decades has undergone an unprecedented process of secularisation. Statistical data leave no doubt as to the extent of the decline of religious belief and practice [15].

A report entitled *Europe's Young Adults and Religion* (2018) based on data from the European social survey 2014-16, by Stephen Bullivant, a professor of theology and the sociology of religion at St Mary's University in London, describes religion in Europe as "moribund". As the report states, "With some notable exceptions young adults increasingly are not identifying with or practising religion."

But to claim that the marginalisation and irrelevance of faith is the inexorable fate of a technologically advanced society is disingenuous. Secularisation, far from the inescapable fate of a modern society, is the intended outcome of a clear ideological agenda, relentlessly pursued by cultural, political and economic forces.

The dismantling of the traditional Christian moral order, the "crusade to liberate the individual from the Western tradition with its Christian moral straitjacket" – as journalist Paul Kelly puts it [16] - and its replacement with an illusory moral system, has been the result of a culture war waged by the advocates of secular ideology, who strive to advance their cause through the media and the educational system.

It is hardly a secret that university campuses have largely become a platform for professors to promote an anti-Christian outlook on history and social issues (abortion, or LGBT ideology, being prime examples); a place where the secularist perspective has become pervasive to the point that it is the only truly viable option, and its tenets are so unquestionable that they are assumed as a matter of course. Any counterargument to the prevailing secular consensus is ignored, and anyone who voices an opinion outside the range of acceptable opinions is censored and ostracized [17].

Indeed, intolerance of those who fail to conform to secular orthodoxy was openly legitimised and encouraged by highly influential ideologues of secularism such as philosopher and political theorist Herbert Marcuse, who in his essay *Repressive tolerance* [18] argues in favour of "new and rigid restrictions on teachings and practices in the educational institutions" as a way to contrast what is perceived as an outdated cultural and moral system.

By achieving what Marxist philosopher Antonio Gramsci defined as "cultural hegemony", the ability to control public discourse "via infiltration of schools, universities, churches and the media", secularists were able to shape public opinion and impose their views upon society [19], and by doing so they influenced the democratic process, perpetuating policies which reinforced the secular perspective. They understood that cultural hegemony inevitably morphs into political hegemony, that cultural change precedes and informs political change.

As David R. Hodge notes, "Through their dominance of the professional landscape —the entertainment industry, news media, education, governmental and regulatory sectors, corporate leadership, and other mainstream, professional venues— secular people play a central role in constructing the narrative that informs the broader society." [20]

And yet, there remains a crucial question: why did secularists' "long march through the institutions" - to borrow a slogan coined by activist Rudi Dutschke - encounter no resistance? Why did Christians fail to stop, much less reverse, the decline of religious influence over culture and society?

As I outlined previously, at the root of secularisation is not merely the non-belief in the existence of God, but the acceptance of the dogma of a morality without God, a set of moral values independent from God, from Christ, who therefore becomes irrelevant.

It would be impossible to decipher the political and social changes that have occurred over the last few decades, without taking into account the assimilation of the central presupposition of secularism by those who were expected to oppose it. As our atheist friend correctly remarks, "the central tenets of secularism … are now widely accepted even amongst believers".

Indeed, the dogma of a morality without God is the assumption that underpins contemporary society. This false premise, which was the prerogative of non-believers, has become conventional wisdom, an unquestionable doctrine accepted as a matter of fact by those who identify as Christians.

The goal of the Philosophes of the Enlightment and their *Encyclopédie* [21], the denial of the transcendent foundation of morality and the attempt to create "a new natural morality as an alternative to the prevailing Christian morality" [22], has become the default position of society, the only acceptable narrative.

The importance of this cannot be over-estimated, because the ideological submission of western Christians has inevitably reverberated in the political sphere, and made possible the legislative framework which has allowed, and at times encouraged, the marginalisation of Christianity.

The left-right paradigm appears increasingly inadequate to

describe the political and cultural battle lines, as parties across the political spectrum subscribe to the same secular premise of a morality without God, and, therefore accept, all the corollaries that proceed from it: the denial of the role of religion and its symbols in the public square, the notion that religion should be exclusively a 'private matter', the absolute separation of government and religion, and the neutrality of the state.

Mainstream conservatism in particular has all but abandoned the Burkean notion of a transcendent, pre-existent morality as the basis of society [23], "an immortal contract between God and man" [24], and become an ideology that panders to political correctness and identity politics: paying lip service to traditional Christian values, but in fact embracing the fashionable orthodoxies of secularism. As a result, the dividing line between Conservatives and Liberals has blurred to a point that it is hardly recognisable.

Political commentator Dennis Prager offers a valuable insight in the mindset of contemporary conservatives, highlighting the substantial alignment of conservative thought with secularist ideology. He recalls: "Many years ago, I attended a dinner at a wealthy man's New York City condo with, among others, one of the most prominent and influential conservatives in American life. ... At one point, the subjects of God and religion came up, and I mentioned how essential God is to morality — that without God, morality is subjective, a matter of personal or communal opinion. ... I was quite surprised when this prominent conservative took strong issue with me: God is morally unnecessary, he stated with some passion — why would any educated person think otherwise?"

Prager concludes: "Most well-educated conservatives have embraced secular values and made peace with a secular and godless America just as much as have well-educated leftists" [25].

The anecdote perfectly captures the defining trait of modern conservatism: unconditional adherence to secular prejudice, wholesale dismissal of the notion of a "transcendent order", preceding and underlying politics, outright rejection of the idea that "morality ... must be supported by the sanction of religious faith, or it cannot stand." [26]

In the words of sociologist Frank Furedi, by accepting the premise of secularism as an irrefutable postulate, conservatives "quietly retreated from the battlefield of culture. The institutions of the media, culture and education did not need to be infiltrated; their previous owners had left the doors wide open" [27].

Above all, the presupposition that religious belief is not the basis of morality, and, therefore, that laws, institutions, society as a whole do not require a transcendent foundation, has led to the denial of any legitimacy to Christianity in the public square.
The insistence on schools as religion-free zones, the hysteria over any reference to religious tradition, the demand for religious symbols to be removed from public spaces, are consequences of the false premise that "God is morally unnecessary".

To turn the tide of secularisation, to reclaim the cultural and political battlefield, is to reject that premise, and to defy the modern false idol of a "morality without God".

CHAPTER 12

SECULARISM AND MULTICULTURALISM

The United Kingdom owes its laws, law-making, customs, traditions and values to the Christian faith. To pretend that this rich heritage can be systematically eradicated in favour of 'multiculturalism' and 'secularism' is a fallacy. There is a myth that politics should be secular and that secularism is somehow neutral. It is not. It has its own dogma, a distinct orthodoxy and an intolerance of dissent every bit as intransigent as those religions it frequently misrepresents and seeks to neuter. Instead of constantly demanding that religion should be removed from politics, perhaps the time has come for there to be a strict separation of secularism and state.

Blogger Cranmer

To argue that morality cannot exist without God equates to implicitly assert the hegemony of Christianity over other faiths and to deny the possibility for the state to be neutral and impartial, and therefore respectful of other beliefs, or the absence of belief. This is in fact an endorsement of theocracy, of a regime where a sort of Christian "sharia law" rules. In a multicultural, multi-faith, pluralist society this is unacceptable. For this reason I believe that the pursuit of absolute separation of government and religion is a fundamental tenet of our society. I find particularly distressful that religious belief is being imposed and has a place in the public square. I'm not out to get rid of religion; I just want to get rid of it from public life. Religion should be a private matter and should not influence public policy.

Let me firstly respond to the remark that "to argue morality cannot exist without God equates to implicitly deny the possibility for the state to be neutral and impartial". Our atheist commentator is absolutely right. The state cannot - outrageous as it might sound to secular, politically correct ears - be neutral, impartial, indifferent towards any belief, because the moral values that sustain society and its institutions are rooted in religious belief. As Ernst-Wolfgang Böckenförde acknowledged, "The liberal secular state lives on premises that it cannot itself guarantee" [28]. The state cannot be "neutral", but it has to recognise and defend its transcendent, religious premise, which, in Western society, is Christianity. The pursuit of absolute separation of government and religion is not – as our atheist claims - a fundamental tenet of our society. It is the secularist delusion of our age [29].

There is of course a corollary to this. Contrary to our atheist's claim that "religion should be a private matter and should not influence public policy", religion, as foundation of culture and moral values, is not and will never be only a private matter. If religion is the basis for morality, it is absurd to maintain that religion is not, and cannot be, a political and social factor. Every political, economic, social argument is at the root a theological argument. Politics and economics are expression of the cultural and therefore religious substrate of society. The denial of the role of religion in the public square originates from failure to understand and/or acknowledge why religion has such a role.

Does the recognition of the role of Christianity as the ultimate source of moral principles inevitably lead to a theocratic regime, disrespectful of other beliefs, or the absence of belief? The answer is no. For the simple reason that the distinction between temporal and spiritual powers is itself a product of Christianity, not of secularism. Moral nothingness cannot create anything, not even this distinction.

Interestingly, in order to exemplify a political system where the distinction between religion and politics is absent, our atheist uses an expression that is alien to Christian doctrine and tradition: "sharia law". Islam is a political system, where religion and state coincide [30]. Christianity is not. Dinesh D'Souza notes:

> For centuries the kings and the church fought over how to draw the legitimate dividing line between the two spheres, but both sides agreed that there was a dividing line. [31]

The reason of this uniqueness is Christian belief itself, which is not primarily a divinely revealed law that can be mechanically translated into civil law, but it is God Himself, the Reason of the Law who becomes flesh, and as such cannot be identified with the law of the state. The heterogeneity between God made flesh and civil law has produced the distinction between political and spiritual spheres. This extraordinary and entirely new theological concept has shaped Western societies to this day.

Secularism on the other hand is a moral vacuum, and to claim that we can lay the foundations of our society, of any society, on this vacuum is nonsense. The moral principles atheists take for granted do not spring from secularism, but from the religious tradition they, consciously or not, belong to. Daniel P. Moloney defines this position as "moral parasitism":

> When atheists reject the religion in which they have been raised, they tend to keep the morality while

discarding its theological foundation. Their ethical behaviour is then derivative and parasitic, borrowing its conscience from a culture permeated by religion; it cannot survive if the surrounding religious culture is not sustained. In short, morality as we know it cannot be maintained without Judeo-Christian religion. [32]

The supposed "secular" values atheists hold dear are in fact borrowed Christian values. Our society is respectful of any creed, or lack thereof, not because it embraces an illusory, non-existent secular morality, but because it is rooted in Christian faith. Christopher Dawson noted that "we cannot understand the inner form of a society unless we understand its religion." [33] Because moral values are always a religious product, and Western moral values are a product of Christianity [34]. Our values, what we believe has a value beyond and above our self-interest, are grounded in religious faith or are not grounded at all.

As T. S. Eliot reminds us in his *Notes Towards the Definition of Culture* (1948):

> An individual European may not believe that the Christian Faith is true, and yet what he says, and makes, and does, will all spring out of his heritage of Christian culture and depend upon that culture for its meaning. Only a Christian culture could have produced a Voltaire or a Nietzsche. I do not believe that the culture of Europe could survive the complete disappearance of the Christian Faith... If Christianity goes, the whole of our culture goes.

Which brings me to the subject of multiculturalism. When our atheist uses the term "multiculturalism", he doesn't merely describe a social phenomenon. He actually states an ideological position based on the atheist dogma that morality can exist without God; that man does not need God, because he can create his own "neutral" set of moral values, an autonomous entity detached from any religious source, opposed to religious moral values. Multiculturalism as ideological category is precisely the by-product of this false premise. It is the ideology of cultural and religious indifference, which denies the transcendent origin of the moral values that form the basis of our civilisation, and therefore implies the irrelevance of religion. Multiculturalism is the choice not to have a culture, because choosing a culture implicitly means to choose a religion. It is the assertion that Christianity, or any religious faith, is irrelevant and can be easily and harmlessly disposed of, because a supposedly "secular set of values" is ready to take its place. Which is, as I said, a fallacy. "Morality without God", a moral common denominator independent from all creeds, does not exist, other than in the minds of secular ideologues.

The "neutrality" heralded by secularism is in fact a biased, prejudiced anti-religious position, based on the ideologically motivated refusal to acknowledge that religion is the basis for morality. As G.K. Chesterton argued, "There are those who hate Christianity and call their hatred an all-embracing love for all religions."

It is ironic that this secular prejudice has been in a way exposed by Islamic countries' failure to endorse the United Nations' Universal Declaration of Human Rights (UDHR), and their decision to adopt instead the Cairo Declaration on Human Rights in Islam (CDHRI), an alternative declaration which affirms sharia law as the sole source of human rights. Professor Riffat Hassan from the University of Louisville explains:

> What needs to be pointed out to those who uphold the Universal Declaration of Human Rights to be the highest, or sole, model, of a charter of equality and liberty for all human beings, is that given the Western

origin and orientation of this Declaration, the "universality" of the assumptions on which it is based is - at the very least - problematic and subject to questioning. [35]

Muslim countries have emphatically made clear that they do not subscribe to the secular narrative of a "morality without God", a neutral, autonomous entity detached from any religious source. They perceive the principles enshrined in the United Nations' Declaration as an indirect product of the Christian tradition of the West. And they are correct, because that is precisely what these principles are.

The undermining of Christian faith, systematically pursued by Western cultural and political elites, does not lead to some sort of secular Utopia with its own "neutral" morality, but to the rise of religious beliefs other than Christianity, which will bring their own – often opposite - moral values.

On the clean slate of atheism anything can be written, even sharia law.

NOTES

1   "Attempts to derive *ought* from *is* are like attempts to
    reach an odd number by adding together even numbers. If
    someone claims that they've done it, you don't have to
    check their math; you know that they've made a mistake."
    Sean Carroll, *The Big Picture*, 2010

2   *Medea*, Euripides, 431 BC

3   *The Antichrist*, Friedrich Nietzsche, 1895

4   *The Millican Brief*, Peter Hitchens, 2012

5   "Marxism is materialism. As such, it is as relentlessly
    hostile to religion... We must combat religion — that is
    the ABC of all materialism, and consequently of Marxism.
    But Marxism is not a materialism which has stopped at
    the ABC. Marxism goes further. It says: We must know
    how to combat religion, and in order to do so we must
    explain the source of faith and religion among the masses
    in a materialist way. The combating of religion cannot be
    confined to abstract ideological preaching, and it must not
    be reduced to such preaching. It must be linked up with
    the concrete practice of the class movement, which aims
    at eliminating the social roots of religion." Vladimir Ilyich
    Lenin, *The Attitude of the Workers' Party to Religion*, 1909

6   "…almost all those who espouse the relativistic 'methods'
    introduced into the humanities by Foucault, Derrida and
    Rorty are vehement adherents to a code of political
    correctness that condemns deviation in absolute and
    intransigent terms. The relativistic theory exists in order to
    support an absolutist doctrine." Roger Scruton, *Fool, frauds
    and firebrands*, 2015

7   "Political correctness seeks to put boundaries on offensive

speech and behavior; but there is the risk that such boundaries are likely to be determined by the personal beliefs and values of those in power. This means that the definition of what is offensive can change with each group that comes into power." Anne Reynolds, *Political Correctness*, 2009

8   *The Rage Against God*, Peter Hitchens, 2010

9   In August 2014, a woman posed a hypothetical scenario to Richard Dawkins, tweeting: "I honestly don't know what I would do if I were pregnant with a kid with Down syndrome. Real ethical dilemma." Dawkins replied: "Abort it and try again. It would be immoral to bring it into the world if you have the choice."

10 *A Clockwork Orange*, 1971 dystopian crime film adapted, produced, and directed by Stanley Kubrick, based on Anthony Burgess's 1962 novella *A Clockwork Orange*.

11 *Confessions*, Book II, St. Augustine of Hippo, 4th century AD

12 *Escolios a un texto implícito*, Nicolás Gómez Dávila, 1977

13 *Mere Christianity*, C.S. Lewis, 1952

14 "The singular event which historians use to demarcate the modern era, the French Revolution, was defined by its rejection of religious authority. Since then, secularisation and modernisation have been intimately linked in the minds of many. All three 'founding fathers' of sociological theory - Marx, Weber and Durkheim - cast a narrative of modernisation in which religion was an inevitable casualty of advancing rationality." Eric Kaufmann, *The End of Secularisation in Europe? A Demographic Perspective*, 2012

15 "Over the last decades for which data is available, both self-identified Christians and those who regularly attend church services plummeted throughout most of the

continent. The Center for the Study of Global Christianity at Gordon Conwell Theological Seminary predicts that five years from now, the number of Christians in Western Europe will have fallen by almost 23 percent since 1970. And actual attendance is abysmal, with less than 2 percent of the population darkening the door of a church on a regular basis in Britain, France, or Germany. According to the European Values Study as reported by The Christian Post, half of the population in many areas of Europe never attend religious services. And Germany, a country with one-quarter the population of the United States, is home to 10 times as many atheists. The Church of England is now closing around 20 churches a year, and about 200 churches in Denmark have been deemed non-viable by their parishes over the past 10 years. An estimated 515 Roman Catholic churches in Germany have closed their doors over the same period, and most shockingly, Catholic clergy estimate that two-thirds of their 1,600 churches in the Netherlands will be closed by 2020." Shane Morris, *Europe's abandoned churches a warning for America*, 2015

16   *New progressive morality rapidly taking over from Christian beliefs*, Paul Kelly, The Australian, 15 April 2017

17   "Secular perspectives are presented as normative. When religion is presented, it is depicted in a manner that reflects the concerns of secular elites. Traditional spiritual leaders are framed as outdated, out of touch, and often dangerous individuals who need to be challenged for the benefit of society. Positive portrayals that reflect the views of people of faith are rare, if not nonexistent. A search of 20 years of programming failed to reveal any scripts that affirmed the importance of faith, the possibility of miracles, or the power of prayer (Lichter et al., 1994)" David R. Hodge PhD, *Secular Privilege: Deconstructing the Invisible Rose-Tinted Sunglasses*, Journal of Religion &

Spirituality in Social Work, 2009

18   *Repressive tolerance, Postscript,* Herbert Marcuse, 1968

19   "There exists an international subculture composed of people with Western-type higher education, especially in the humanities and social sciences, that is indeed secularised. This subculture is the principal "carrier" of progressive, Enlightened beliefs and values. While its members are relatively thin on the ground, they are very influential, as they control the institutions that provide the "official" definitions of reality, notably the educational system, the media of mass communication, and the higher reaches of the legal system." Peter Berger, *Secularism in retreat,* 1996

20   *Secular Privilege: Deconstructing the Invisible Rose-Tinted Sunglasses,* Journal of Religion & Spirituality in Social Work, David R. Hodge PhD, 2009

21   *L'Encyclopédie,* Denis Diderot and Jean D'Alembert, Paris, 1762-72

22   *The French Revolution,* J. F. Bosher, New York, 1988

23   "We know, and what is better, we feel inwardly, that religion is the basis of civil society, and the source of all good and of all comfort." Edmund Burke, *Reflections on the French Revolution,* 1790

24   *The Intelligent Woman's Guide to Conservatism,* Russell Kirk, 1957

25   *Conservatives, Too, Undergo Secular Indoctrination,* Dennis Prager, RealClearPolitics, 03 April 2008

26   Russell Kirk, arguably the most influential conservative thinker of the 20th century, identifies the essence of conservatism in the idea of society as "spiritual reality", in the conviction that our purpose in this world is "not to

indulge our appetites, but to render obedience to divine ordinance" (*The Conservative Mind*, 1953), and declares that "there could be no conservatism without a religious foundation, and it is conservative people, by and large, who defend religion in our time." (*Russell Kirk's Concise Guide to Conservatism*, 2019). In Kirk's eyes, hostility or indifference towards religion, and "obsession with economic objects", epitomised by Bentham's utilitarianism, disqualify from the definition of conservatism. Indeed, he considers the reduction of the individual to mere *homo oeconomicus*, a purely material entity devoid of spiritual dimension, as a form of proto-Marxism.

27 *1968: The birth of the new conformism*, Frank Furedi, Spiked, 30 May 2018

28 *Staat, Gesellschaft, Freiheit*, Ernst-Wolfgang Böckenförde, 1976

29 The phrase "wall of separation between Church and State" first appears in a letter Thomas Jefferson, the third President of the United States of America, wrote in 1802 to the Danbury Baptist Association, and it merely reflects his personal opinion on religious policies. And yet, "today, Jefferson's 'separation between Church & State' terminology has become rooted in the vocabulary of many Americans", who "may go as far as to think that Jefferson's phrase is - and always has been- a part of the constitutional text" (Tara Ross and Joseph C. Smith, *Under God. George Washington and the question of Church and state*, 2008).

Until 1947, jurisprudence unequivocally maintained Christian faith as the bedrock of society. On February 29, 1892, the Supreme Court declared that the historical record of America overwhelmingly demonstrated that the United States "… is a Christian nation." "We are a

Christian people, and the morality of the country is deeply engrafted upon Christianity" (*Holy Trinity v. United States*). A previous ruling by Illinois Supreme Court, (*Richmond v. Moore*, 1883) reads: "Our laws and our institutions must necessarily be based upon and embody the teachings of the Redeemer of mankind. [It is] impossible that it should be otherwise and in the sense and to this extent our civilization and our institutions are emphatically Christian." In his *Commentaries on the Constitution* (1833), Justice Joseph Story, who served on the Supreme Court from 1811 to 1845, writes: "There never has been a period, in which the Common Law did not recognize Christianity as lying at its foundations". "There will probably be found few persons in this, or any other Christian country, who would deliberately contend, that it was unreasonable, or unjust to foster and encourage the Christian religion generally, as a matter of sound policy, as well as of revealed truth. In fact, every American colony, from its foundation down to the revolution… did openly, by the whole course of its laws and institutions, support and sustain, in some form, the Christian religion; and almost invariably gave a peculiar sanction to some of its fundamental doctrines."

This constant interpretation of the Constitution came to an end in 1947, when the US Supreme Court (*Everson v Board of education*) overturned the previous jurisprudence and adopted Jefferson's position, declaring: "The First Amendment has erected a wall between church and state. That wall must be kept high and impregnable. We could not approve the slightest breach." The underlying assumption here is that moral principles upon which society is based do not require a transcendent foundation, and therefore Christianity is no longer the reference point in American society. By embracing Jefferson's view, the Supreme Court validated and officialised the secular perspective, endorsing an ideological interpretation of the constitutional text in order to advance and encourage the secularisation process.

30   "We are accustomed to talking of church and state, and a whole series of pairs of words that go with them – lay and ecclesiastical, secular and religious, spiritual and temporal, and so on. These pairs of words simply do not exist in classical Islamic terminology, because the dichotomy that these words express is unknown. They are used in the modern languages. In Arabic, they borrow the terminology used by Christian Arabs. They are fortunate in having a substantial Christian population using Arabic, and they therefore have a good part of the modern terminology at their disposal, in their own language." Bernard Lewis, *Islam and the West: A Conversation with Bernard Lewis*, Pew research center, 2006

31   *What's So Great about Christianity*, Dinesh D'Souza, 2008

32   *American Prospect*, Daniel P. Moloney, quoted at http://stephenlaw.blogspot.co.uk/2007/04/dependence-of-morality-on-religion.html

33   *Religion and Culture*, Christopher Dawson, 1948

34   "The idea that people have some rights just because they are human, and entirely irrespective of merit, certainly isn't derived from observation of the world. It arose out of Christianity, no matter how much Christians have in practice resisted it. Although human rights have become embedded in our institutions at the same time as religious observance has been in decline, they could become vulnerable in an entirely post-Christian environment where the collective memory slips from the old moorings inherited from Christian ethics." *The Guardian view on disappearing Christianity: suppose it's gone for ever?* The Guardian, 27 May 2016

ABOUT THE AUTHOR

Giorgio Roversi was born in Italy, graduated in Law from the University of Parma and now lives in England with his wife and two daughters.

Printed in Great Britain
by Amazon

54178400R00043